T0309452

Wo
Architekten
arbeiten

Where
Architects
Work

Wo
Architekten
arbeiten

NILS BALLHAUSEN (ED.)

BIRKHÄUSER, BASEL | BAUWELT, BERLIN

Where
Architects
Work

Wie sieht es eigentlich bei denen aus, die täglich über gutes Bauen nachdenken? Um das herauszufinden, hat die *Bauwelt* im Sommer 2012 über zweihundert Architekten gebeten, der Redaktion dreierlei zuzusenden: eine Fotografie des Gebäudes, in dem sich das Büro befindet, ein Innenraumfoto sowie eine Grundrisszeichnung, in der die Arbeitsplätze der Inhaber markiert sind. Der Rücklauf sprengte den Umfang einer Wochenzeitschrift. Auch deswegen gibt es dieses Buch.

Schon bei der ersten Durchsicht des Materials fiel auf, dass die Innenaufnahmen – unabhängig von der Lage und Größe der Büros – gar nicht leicht auseinander zu halten sind. Zu ähnlich ist deren Ausstattung, zu verwandt die Atmosphäre. Als habe sich die Architektenschaft auf ein international gültiges Corporate Design verständigt. Das mag einerseits an unserer Auswahl liegen, andererseits dürften berufsspezifische Faktoren, die gereihte Arbeitstische, Modellbaulager, Mustersammlungen oder Hängeflächen verlangen, und „moderne" Codes wie offene Räume, klare Linien und weiße Oberflächen zu räumlichen Lösungen geführt haben, die sich oft nur in Nuancen unterscheiden.

Grafisch vereinheitlicht und im Maßstab 1:333 abgebildet, ermöglichen die Grundrisszeichnungen einen direkten Vergleich. Uns interessierte dabei, wie die Architekturbüros organisiert sind, welcher räumlichen Struktur sie gehorchen und welchen Platz die Inhaber und Inhaberinnen darin einnehmen.

Hervorragende Bauwerke lassen sich offenbar im Wolkenkratzer ebenso erdenken wie in einer hergerichteten Scheune. Die Außenaufnahmen der Gebäude hätten die

How do things actually look where people spend their days thinking about good architecture? In the summer of 2012, in an attempt to find out, *Bauwelt* asked more than two hundred architects to submit three different items to our editorial office: a photograph of the building where his or her office is found; an interior photograph of the office itself; and a floor plan indicating the work space. The responses exceeded the dimensions of a weekly magazine—which is one reason for the present book.

An initial examination of the submitted material revealed that the interior photographs were—leaving aside the question of the respective office's location and size—not easy to tell apart. The furnishings are too similar, the atmosphere too closely related as though the architects had collectively agreed upon an internationally valid corporate design. On the one hand, this may be due to our selection, while on the other, occupation-specific factors may require rows of worktables, storage depots for models, collections of prototypes, and wall surfaces for display purposes, while modernist codes such as open spaces, clear lines, and white surfaces may have led to spatial solutions that are distinguishable only in their nuances.

Unified in terms of presentation and illustrated on a scale of 1:333, the floor plans permit direct comparisons. We were interested in particular in the way in which these architectural offices were organized, in the spatial structures to which they conformed, and in the places their users occupied within them.

Apparently, outstanding buildings can be conceived in skyscrapers just as easily as in renovated barns. The photographs of the exteriors

„ortlosen" Interieurs und die Zeichnungen eigentlich nur begleiten sollen. Vielleicht sind sie es aber, die die Unterschiedlichkeit der Büros am besten illustrieren. Die Immobilie, in der Architekten arbeiten und Geschäftsbesuch empfangen, hat eine besondere Bedeutung. Sie ist nicht nur ein Gehäuse, sie ist ein Statement. Polyglott, bodenständig, verspielt, nüchtern, trashig, klar, ironisch, ehrlich, unberechenbar – zahllose weitere Attribute mag der Betrachter aus dem Anblick dieser Bauten ableiten und womöglich Rückschlüsse auf das gebaute Werk und auf das Selbstverständnis der darin arbeitenden Architekten ziehen.

Dank der unermüdlichen Recherche von Sebastian Spix ist es nicht bei der Idee zu einem Buch geblieben; Korbinian Kainz hat unsere Materialsammlung zu nun 76 Büros in eine grafische Ordnung gebracht. Besonderer Dank gilt den mitwirkenden Architekten, die uns aufschlussreiche Einblicke in das Wesen und den Arbeitsalltag ihres Berufsstandes gewähren.

Ohne dass wir voneinander wussten, hatten sich Prof. Klaus Jan Philipp, Kyra Bullert, Chrissie Muhr und Raoul Humpert an der Universität Stuttgart fast zur selben Zeit wie wir mit dem „Mythos Architekturatelier" befasst und in der Weißenhofgalerie eine Ausstellung zu diesem Thema kuratiert. Es lag nahe, das Team um einen Essay zu bitten, der die Konstanten und Brüche des Typus „Architekturbüro" ebenso umkreist wie seine mögliche Zukunft.

Nils Ballhausen

of these buildings were actually intended only to supplement the placeless interiors and the drawings. It is perhaps precisely these images, however, that best illustrate the differences between the various offices. A special significance is enjoyed by the buildings within which the architects work, and where they conduct business meetings. The building is more than a mere enclosure, it makes a statement. Polyglot, down-to-earth, playful, sober, trashy, lucid, ironic, sincere, unpredictable: these and countless other attributes will be suggested to viewers by views of the buildings—images that allow us to make inferences concerning both the realized works and the self-images of the architects who work within.

Thanks to the tireless research of Sebastian Spix this book became more than an idea; Korbinian Kainz endowed the material collection documenting more than seventy-six offices with an overarching visual order. Special thanks to the participating architects, who provided illuminating insights into the nature and everyday working reality of their occupation.

Around the time we were preoccupied with *The Myth of the Architect's Studio*, and although we were unaware of one another's activities, professor Klaus Jan Philipp, together with Kyra Bullert, Chrissie Muhr, and Raoul Humpert at Stuttgart University were curating an exhibition on the same topic for the Weißenhofgalerie. The idea occurred to us of asking the team to produce an essay circumscribing the continuities and ruptures affecting the architectural office as a type and speculating on its possible future.

Nils Ballhausen

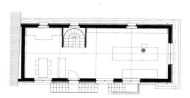

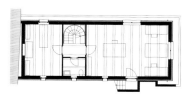

7610 Soglio | Switzerland

Unit 1006, Tower A, Jianwai Soho | 39 Dongsanhuan Zhonglu, Beijing 100022 | China

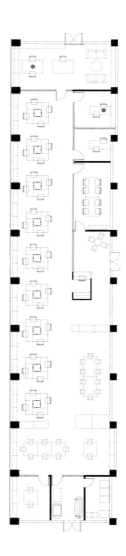

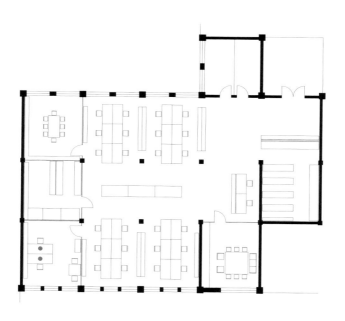

Lindwurmstraße 88 | 80337 München | Germany

Talavera 4 L-5 | 28016 Madrid | Spain

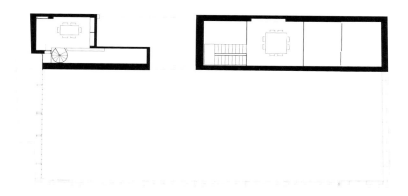

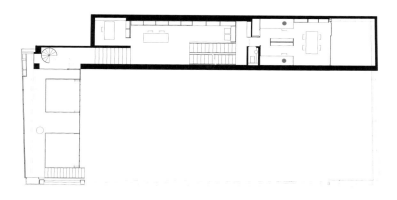

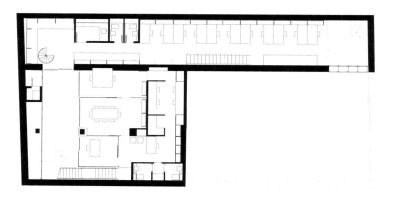

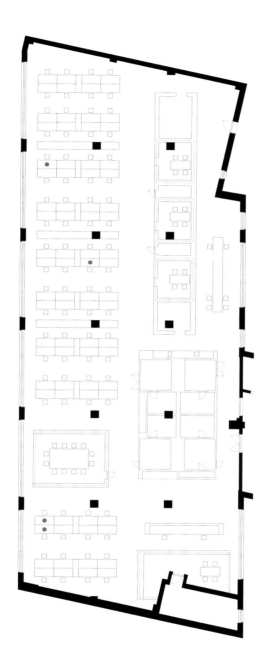

Schlesische Straße 27 | 10997 Berlin | Germany

Krijn Taconiskade 444 | 1087 HW Amsterdam | The Netherlands

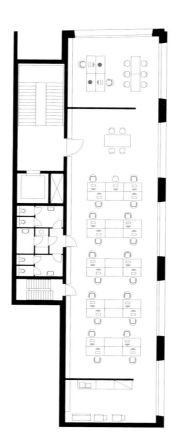

Tivolska 50 | 1000 Ljubljana | Slovenia

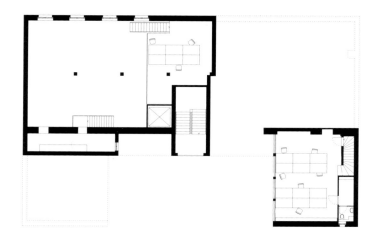

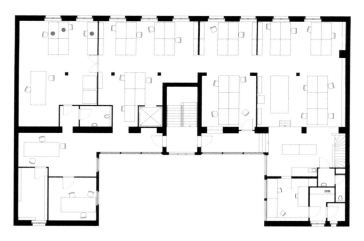

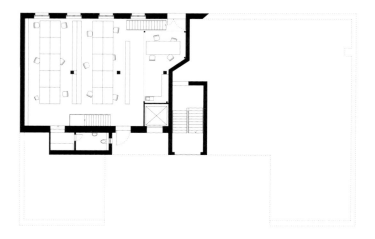

Fischerfeldstraße 13 | 60311 Frankfurt am Main | Germany

Dubsstrasse 45 | 8003 Zürich | Switzerland

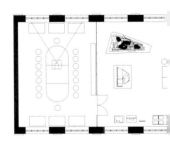

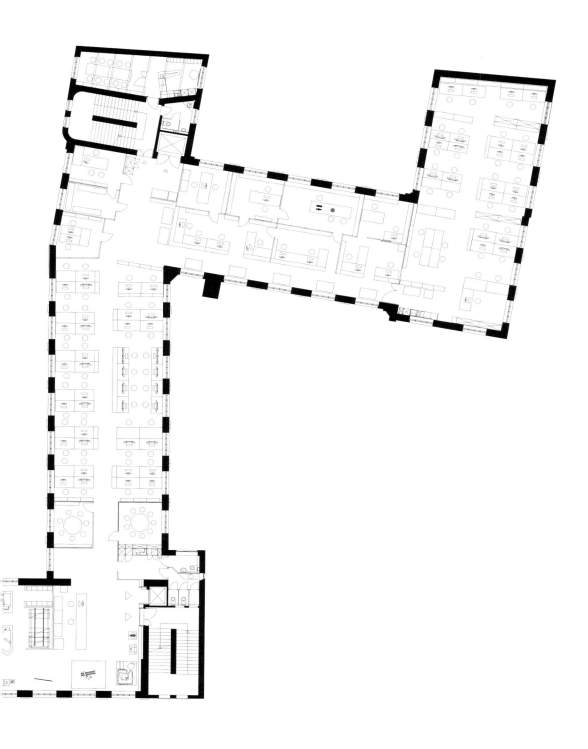

Spengergasse 37 | 1050 Wien | Austria

Oderberger Straße 56 | 10435 Berlin | Germany

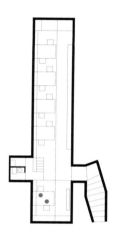

Guecho 27 | 28023 Madrid | Spain

Hüfferstraße 20 | 48149 Münster | Germany

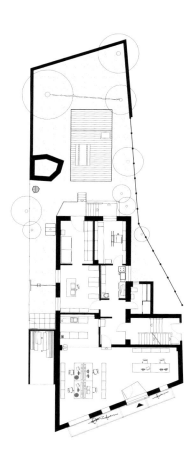

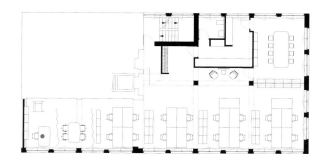

Vorgebirgstraße 338 | 50969 Köln | Germany

Senefelderstraße 77a | 70176 Stuttgart | Germany

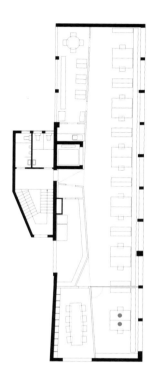

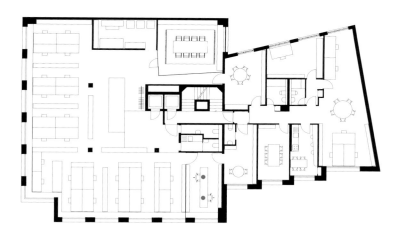

Clarastrasse 2 | 4058 Basel | Switzerland

Elektronstraat 12 | 1014 AP Amsterdam | The Netherlands

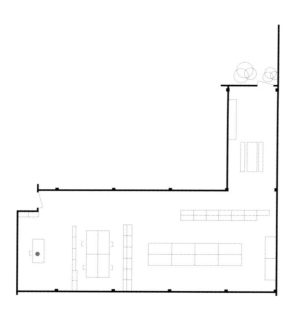

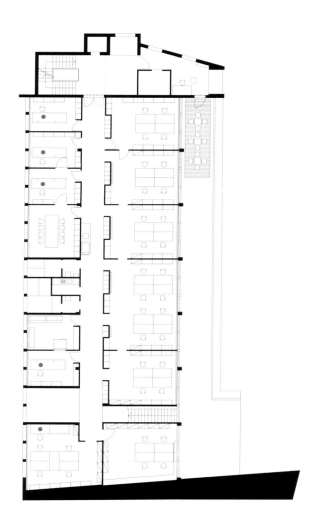

Carmenstrasse 28 | 8032 Zürich | Switzerland

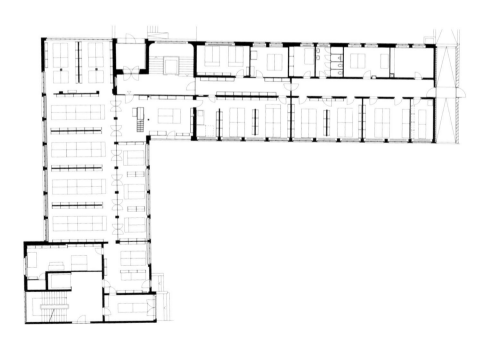

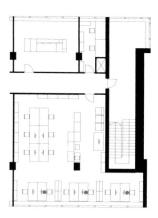

Klosterstraße 44 | 10179 Berlin | Germany

Justinianstraße 16 | 50679 Köln | Germany

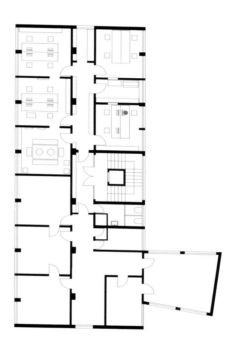

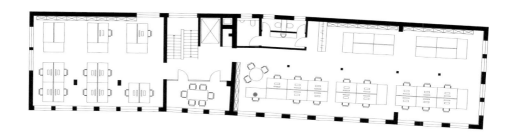

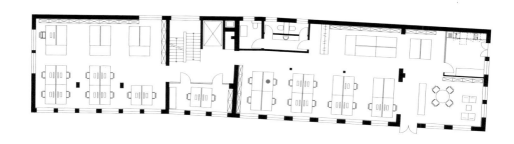

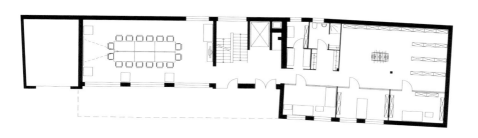

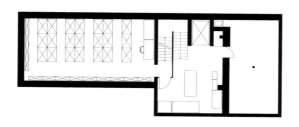

Rotebühlstraße 163a | 70197 Stuttgart | Germany

c/Tafalla 31 Bajo | 31003 Pamplona | Spain

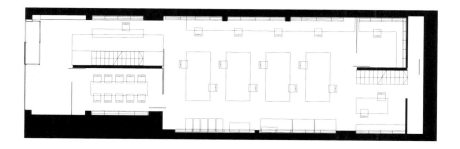

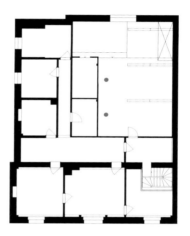

Beethovenstraße 54-56 | 67655 Kaiserslautern | Germany

Köpenicker Straße 48/49d | 10179 Berlin | Germany

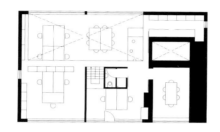

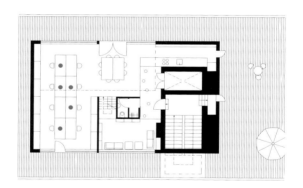

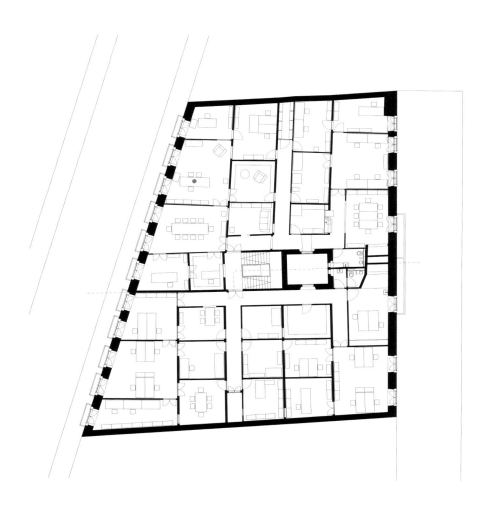

Calçada Marquês de Albrantes, n°48 2°dto | 1200-719 Lisboa | Portugal

Adlerstraße 31 | 70199 Stuttgart | Germany

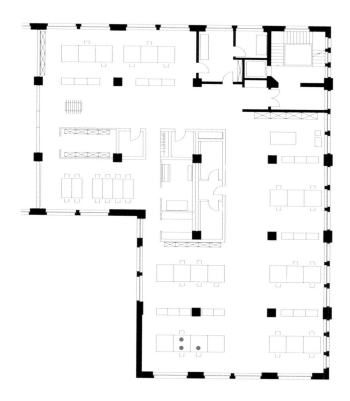

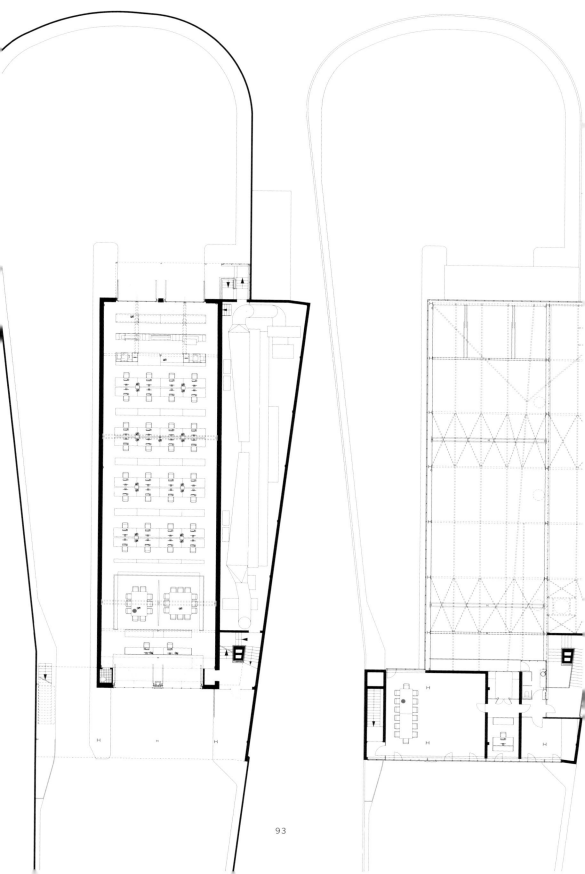

Helmholtzstraße 42 | 10587 Berlin | Germany

Brunnenstraße 9 | 10119 Berlin | Germany

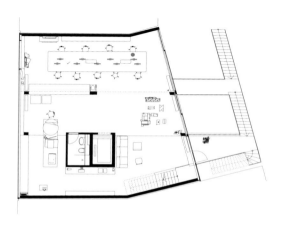

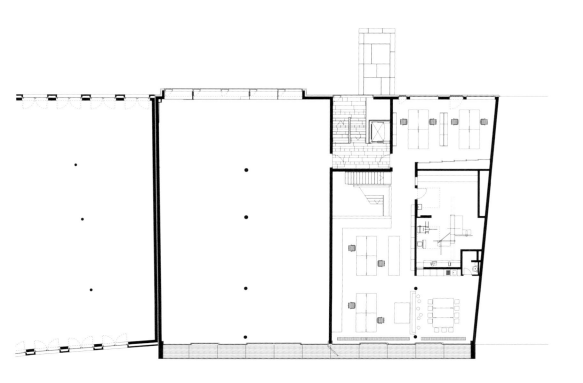

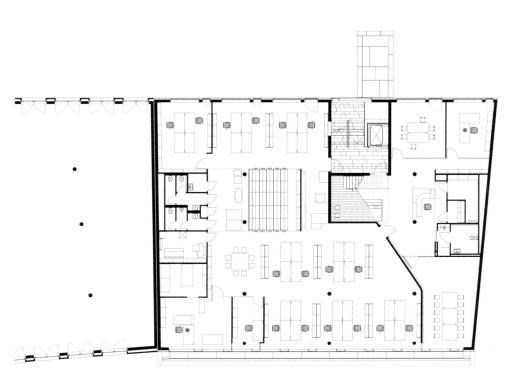

Hafenweg 16 | 48155 Münster | Germany

Kurfürstendamm 173 | 10707 Berlin | Germany

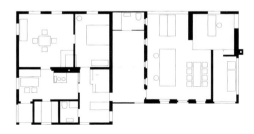

Totengasse 18 | 6833 Weiler | Austria

Bernauer Straße 5d | 10115 Berlin | Germany

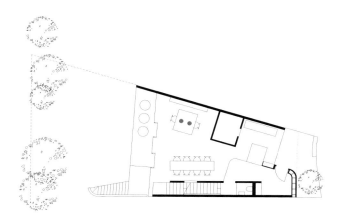

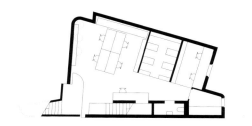

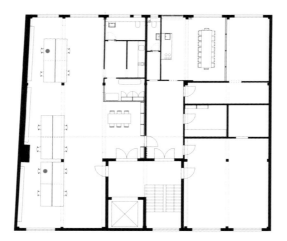

Poststraße 20a | 60329 Frankfurt am Main | Germany

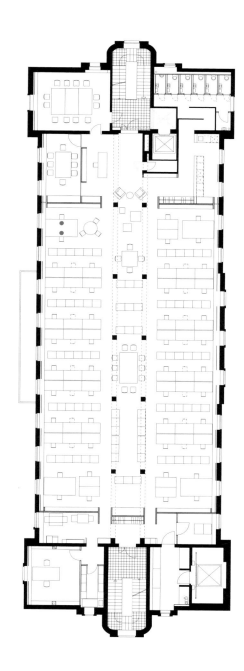

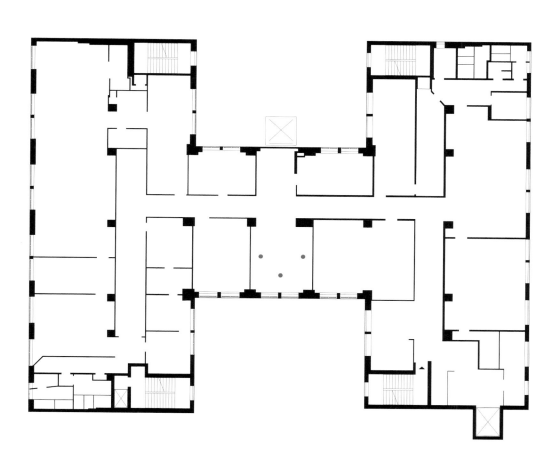

Heidestraße 50 | 10557 Berlin | Germany

Dolomitenweg 19 | 66119 Saarbrücken | Germany

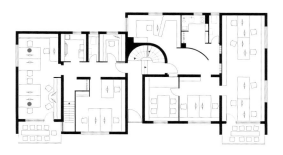

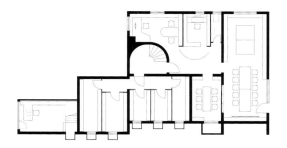

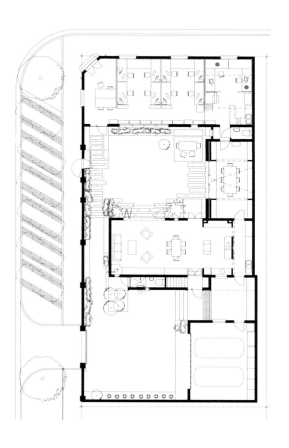

30 Wimbledon Road, corner Barnes Road | Brixton, Johannesburg | South Africa

Van Nelleweg 8065, Building Nr. 8 | 3044 BC Rotterdam | The Netherlands

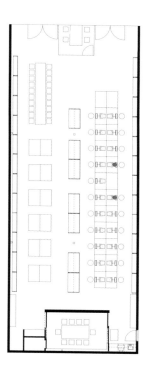

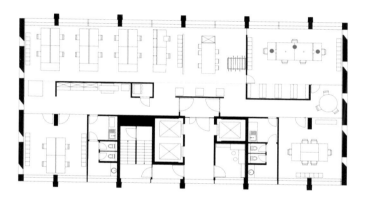

Paul-Nevermann-Platz 5 | 22765 Hamburg | Germany

Michaelisbrücke 1 | 20459 Hamburg | Germany

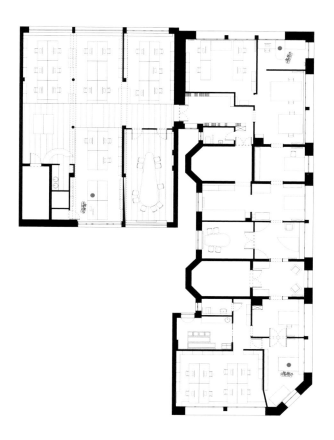

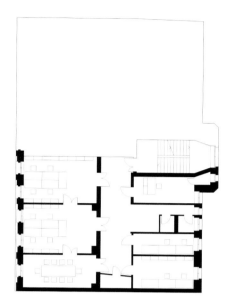

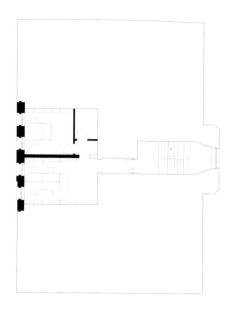

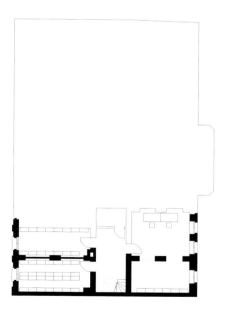

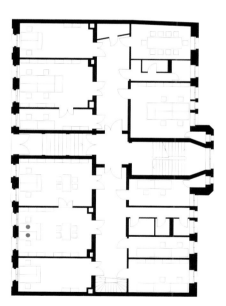

Lampestraße 6 | 04107 Leipzig | Germany

Pfaffendorfer Straße 26b | 04105 Leipzig | Germany

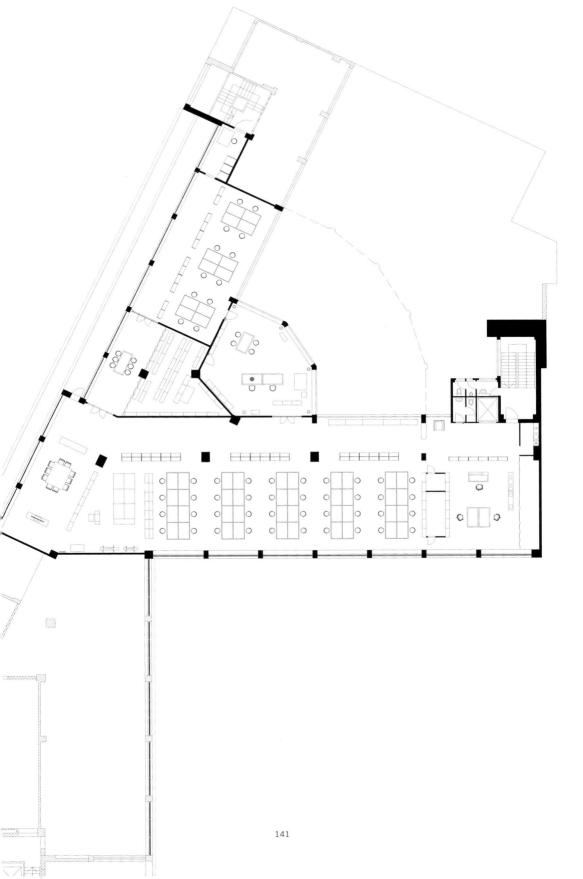

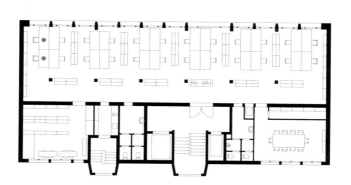

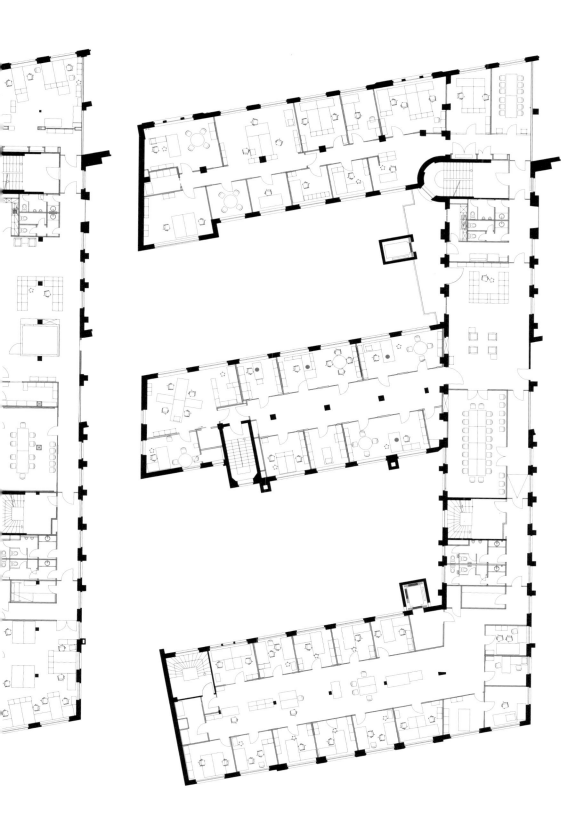

Hedderichstraße 108-110 | 60596 Frankfurt am Main | Germany

Joachimstraße 11 | 10119 Berlin | Germany

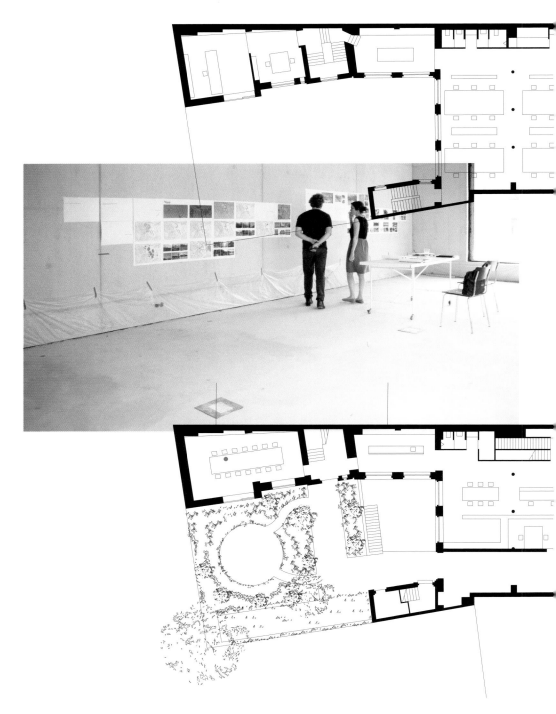

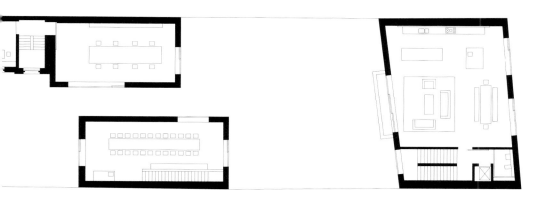

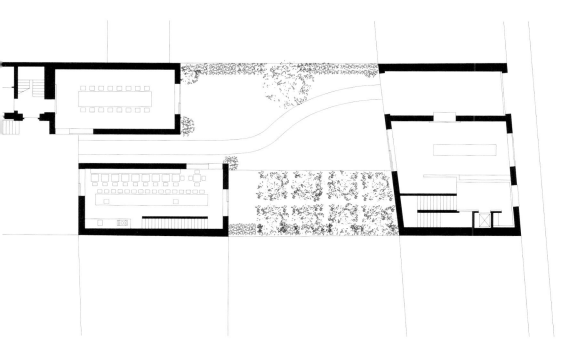

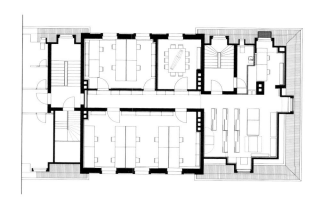

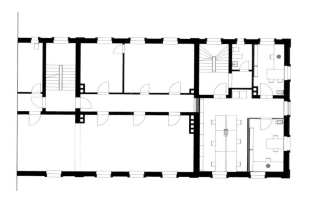

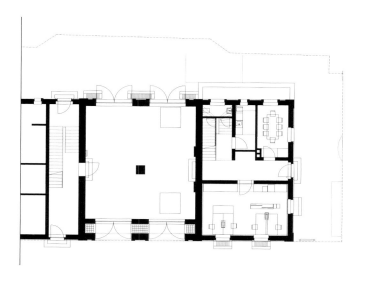

Schulstraße 5 | 80634 München | Germany

Elbchaussee 139 | 22763 Hamburg | Germany

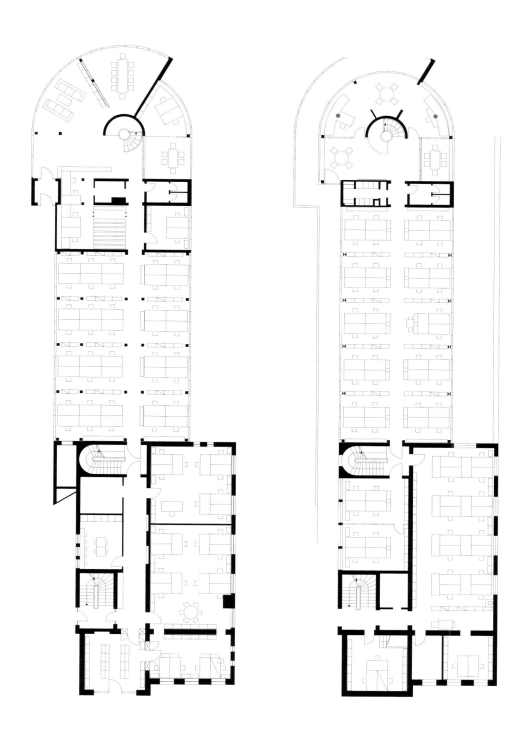

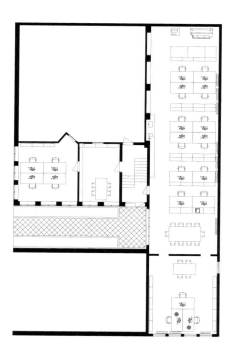

Barer Straße 44 | 80799 München | Germany

36, rue des Jeûneurs | 72002 Paris | France

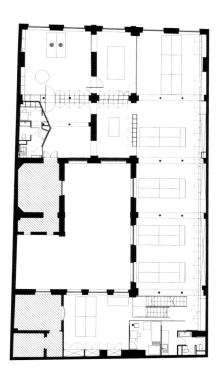

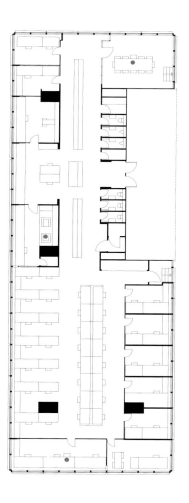

Platz der Republik 6 | 60325 Frankfurt am Main | Germany

Peterstraße 38 | 26121 Oldenburg | Germany

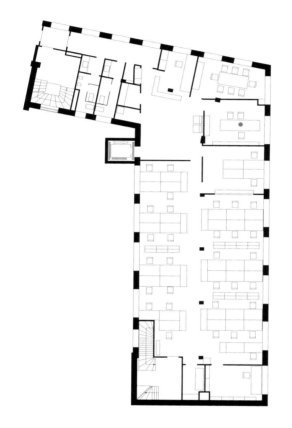

Hedderichstraße 108-110 | 60596 Frankfurt am Main | Germany

Ankerstrasse 3 | 8004 Zürich | Switzerland

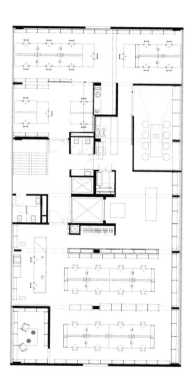

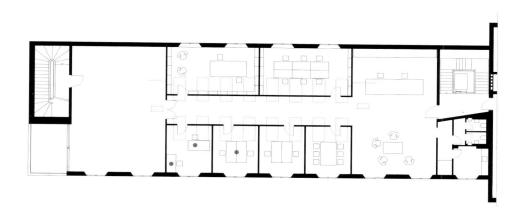

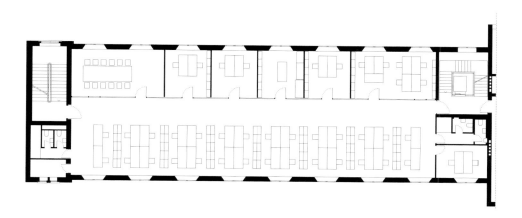

Lehrter Straße 57 | 10557 Berlin | Germany

Kellerstraße 39 | 81667 München | Germany

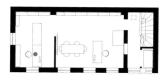

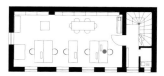

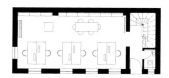

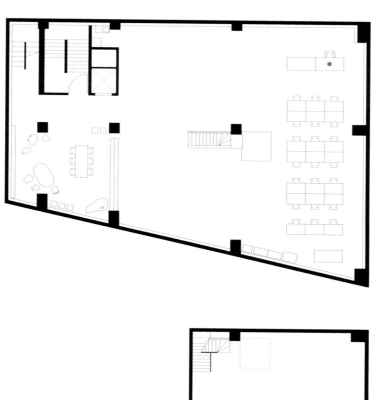

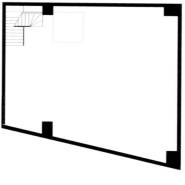

3-18-12 Roppongi, Minato-Ku | Tokio #106-0032 | Japan

© 2013 Google. Image Date: December 2009

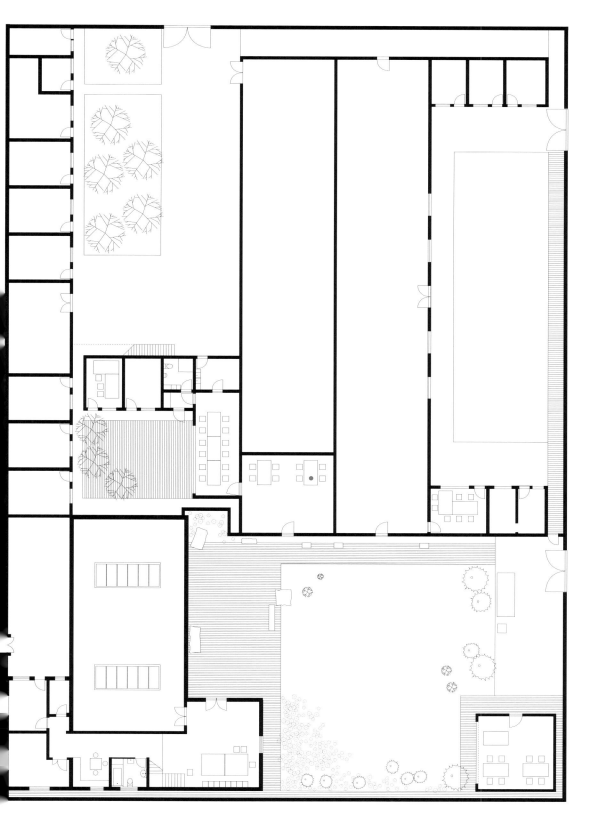

8, rue du Pré aux Clercs | 75007 Paris | France

2 Rector Street, 19th Floor | New York, NY 10006 | United States of America

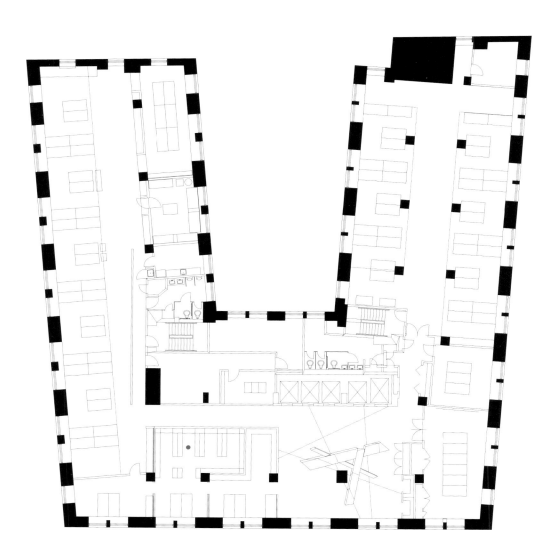

193

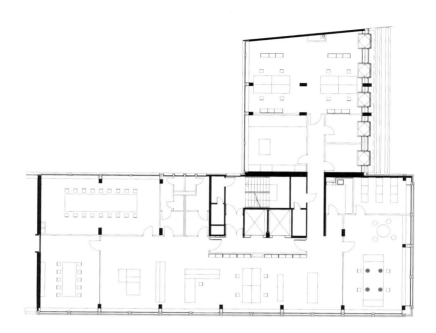

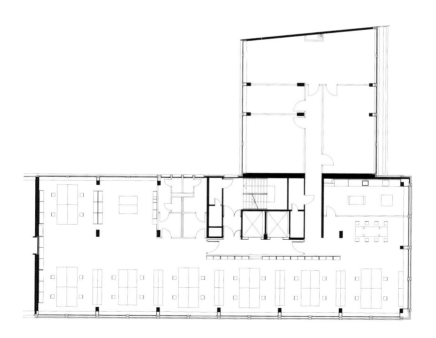

Untere Donaustraße 13 -15 | 1020 Wien | Austria

Schillerstraße 94 | 10625 Berlin | Germany

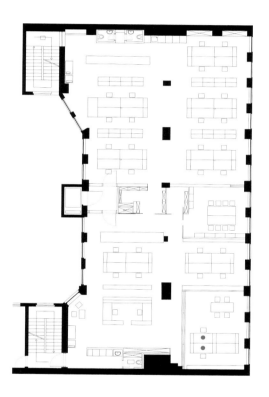

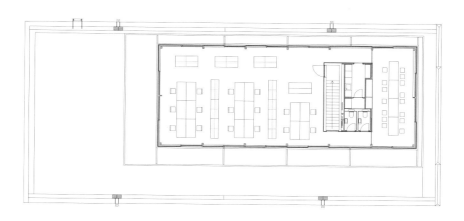

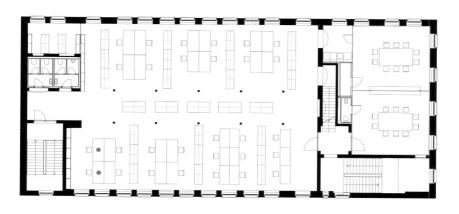

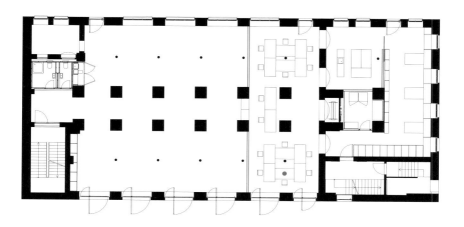

Nymphenburger Straße 125 | 80636 München | Germany

Hardturmstrasse 76 | 8005 Zürich | Switzerland

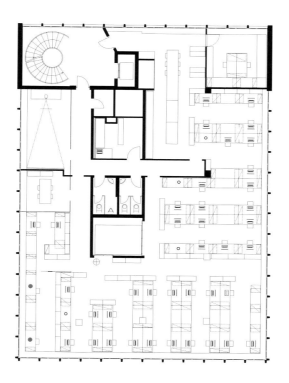

Süsswinkelgasse 10 | 7000 Chur | Switzerland

Renthof 1 | 34117 Kassel | Germany

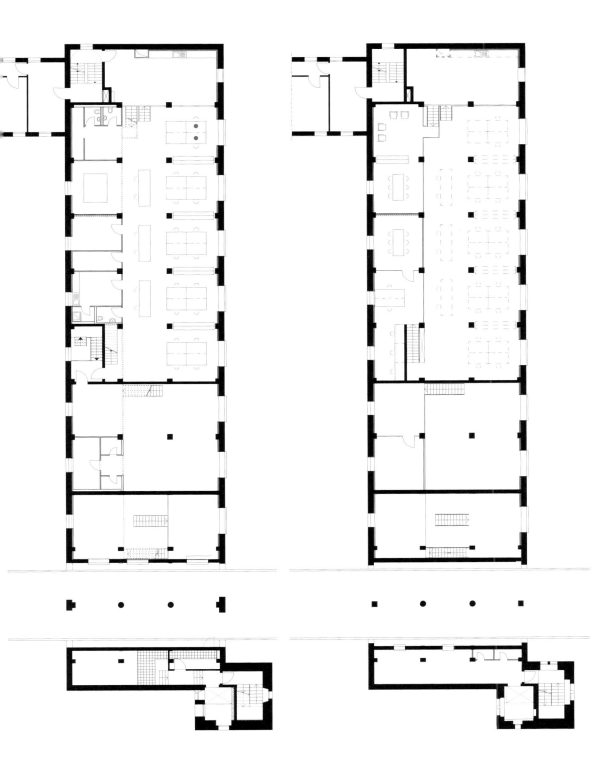

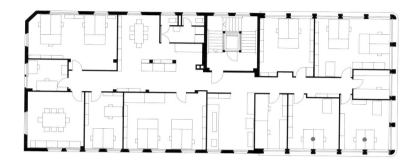

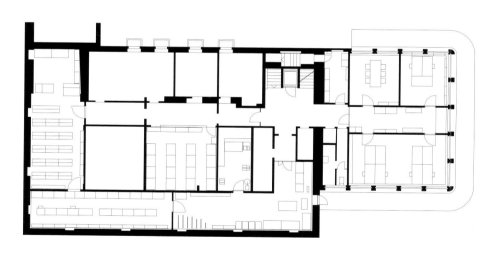

Rykestraße 2. 2. HH | 10405 Berlin | Germany

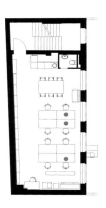

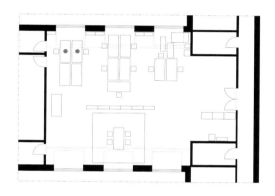

Brunnenstraße 188, Aufgang 2, 5.OG | 10119 Berlin | Germany

Kurfürstendamm 58 | 10707 Berlin | Germany

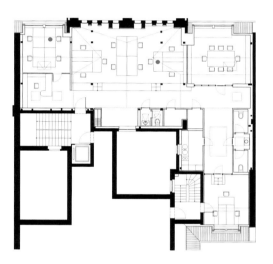

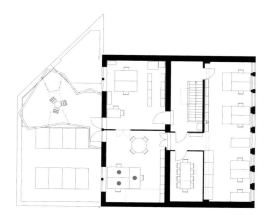

Allschwilerstrasse 71a | 4055 Basel | Switzerland

450 West 31st Street, 11th Floor | New York, NY 10001 | United States of America

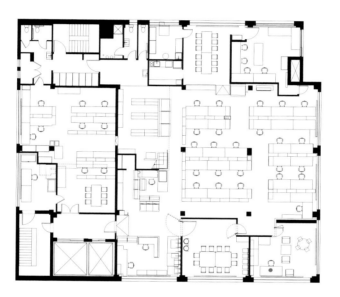

10th Street New Naccache | Beirut | Lebanon

Mumhane Caddesi 18, 3rd Floor | 34425 Karaköy, Istanbul | Turkey

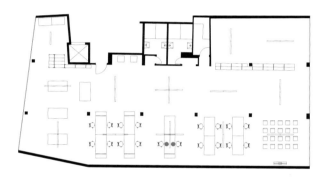

Mythos
Architekturatelier

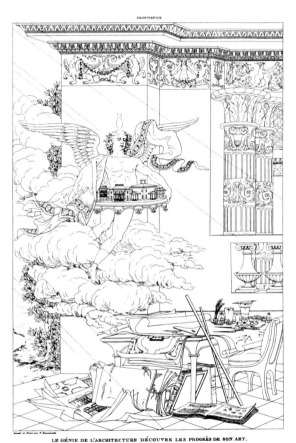

LE GÉNIE DE L'ARCHITECTURE DÉCOUVRE LES PROGRÈS DE SON ART.

*Kyra Bullert, Raoul Humpert, Chrissie Muhr
und Klaus Jan Philipp*

Das Atelier:
Ort für den Genius
der Architektur

Der Stuhl des Architekten ist frei. Wir sind eingeladen, uns zu setzen. Unser Handwerkszeug, die Pläne in der Mappe und auf dem Boden, auch das aufgeschlagene Geometriebuch brauchen wir nicht zu beachten. Der umwölkte, uns von links oben zuschwebende Genius der Architektur präsentiert auf vorgehaltenem Tablett das, wonach wir suchen: Gute, vorbildliche Architektur!

Der Ort, auf dem Frontispiz eines Buches über moderne französische Architektur des Jahres 1801 zu finden, ist ein ideales Architektenatelier. Ein Ort nämlich, an dem einem die Ideen zufliegen! Arbeit bleibt freilich noch genug: Zirkel, Lineale, Stifte, Planmappen und Fachbücher müssen eingesetzt werden, um aus der Idee Wirklichkeit, Gebautes werden zu lassen.

Auch wenn der Zeichner es im Unklaren belässt, welche Gestalt dieses Atelier hat, so gibt es doch einige Hinweise darauf, was für ein ideales Atelier unverzichtbar ist: Arbeitstisch und Stuhl entsprechen der neusten Mode, ebenso die Kandelaber und das Empire-Gebälk des Interieurs. Der Architekt, der sich hier niederlässt, ist *up to date*. Zugleich weiß er, woran er sich letztlich zu orientierten hat, sein Blick geht hinaus in die Natur, die in Gestalt eines unbeschnittenen Lorbeerbaums durchaus doppeldeutig zu verstehen ist.

Das Atelier ist ebenso ein Ort der Sehnsucht wie der Arbeit: Hier fließen Schweiß und Tränen. Tränen der Trauer und Tränen

The Studio:
a Place for Genius
in Architecture

The architect's chair is empty. We are invited to take a seat. We need not attend to the tools of the trade, the plans held in the portfolio on the floor, the opened geometry book. On a tray reserved for the purpose, surrounded by clouds, the genius of architecture—who hovers above on the upper left—presents that for which we are searching: high-quality, exemplary architecture!

This setting—depicted on the frontispiece of a book on modern French architecture that appeared in 1801—is an idealized architectural studio. A place, namely, where ideas simply fly into one's head! Admittedly, there is plenty of work to be done nonetheless: a compass and straightedge, pens, portfolios of plans, and reference books must be deployed before built reality can emerge from the idea.

And although the artist leaves the actual shape of this room ambiguous, there are sufficient indications of the indispensable features of such an ideal studio: the worktable and the chair correspond to the latest fashion, as does the candelabra and the interior's Empire-era woodwork. The architect who occupies this space is up-to-date. At the same time he is aware of the necessary focus of his ultimate orientation—his gaze passes outward toward nature, present in the form of an untrimmed laurel tree whose intended significance remains thoroughly ambiguous.

The studio is a place of yearning as well as of work: flowing here are both sweat and tears. Tears of sorrow or tears of joy—when a compe-

des Glücks, wenn der Wettbewerb gewonnen, der Auftrag ergattert ist. Wo auch immer die besten Ideen entstehen, das Atelier ist der Ort, an dem sie zu konkreten Projekten werden. Ob groß oder klein, ob eine Halle marktähnlicher Ausmaße oder ein winziges *studiolo*, immer ist das Atelier Ort des kreativen Austausches. Hier wird entworfen, verworfen, diskutiert, gefeiert, gelacht und geweint.

Die Einheit von Atelier und Stil

Eine architektonische Typologie des Ateliers gibt es nicht. Im Unterschied zum klassischen Künstleratelier braucht es kein großes Fenster mit Nordlicht, es braucht keine große Höhe, keine weite Fläche. Es kann ein einfacher, schlauchartiger Raum sein wie Le Corbusiers Atelier in der Rue de Sèvres in Paris oder ein komplexes Raumprogramm wie bei Frank Lloyd Wrights Taliesin. Das Architekturatelier kann sich irgendwo einhausen, in einer Etagenwohnung, im ehemaligen Eckgeschäft oder in einer Industriehalle. Manche Architekten beginnen im Souterrain. Erfolgreiche Büros präsentieren sich im eigenen Haus, das auch mal ein Schiff sein kann.

Als Ideal gilt die Deckungsgleichheit von Atelier und Haltung des jeweiligen Büros. Das Atelier wird dann zur Visitenkarte des Architekten. Über die Ateliers der Architekten von der Antike bis ins 20. Jahrhundert wissen wir recht wenig. Von manchen kennen wir das eigene Haus, das auch einen Arbeitsplatz für den Bauherrn und seine Mitarbeiter vorsieht. Doch ist hier der Wohnzweck meist höher gewichtet, womit solche Häuser eher zur

tition entry is victorious, a commission is landed. No matter whence the best ideas emerge, the studio is the place where they are translated into specific projects. Whether as large as a market hall or as small as a tiny *studiolo*, the studio is always the place of creative exchange. Here the architect designs, rejects, discusses, celebrates, laughs, and cries.

The Unity of Studio and Style

There is nothing like an architectural typology of the studio. In contradistinction to the classical artist's studio, the architect requires no large window with light from the north; nor is exceptional height necessary, nor particularly large dimensions. His studio can be a simple, tunnel-shaped space like Le Corbusier's workroom on the rue de Sèvres in Paris, or a complex spatial program like Frank Lloyd Wright's Taliesin. The architect's studio can be accommodated almost anywhere: in an apartment, in a former corner shop, or in an industrial hall. Some architects begin in the basement. Successful offices occupy their own buildings—which may even be found on ships.

The ideal is a relationship of correspondence between the style of the studio and the attitude of the respective architectural practice. The studio then becomes the architect's calling card. We know rather little about the architect's studio from antiquity up to the twentieth century. For some architects we know their homes, envisioned as work spaces for both the owner and his colleagues. But in such instances the requirements of residence were accorded priority, assigning such buildings to the

Pompeji in München: Leo von Klenzes Atelier gezeichnet von Christian Jank
Pompeii in Munich: Leo von Klenze's studio, depicted by Christian Jank

Typologie der Künstlerhäuser als zu unserem Thema gehören.

Betrachten wir das Atelier ausschließlich als Binnenraum innerhalb einer vorgegebenen Hausstruktur, so gilt dennoch derselbe Anspruch wie an ein Künstlerhaus. Möblierung und Ausstattung sollen dem entsprechen, was der Architekt seinen Auftraggebern vermitteln will, das, wofür er „steht", eine Widerspiegelung seines Geschmacks, seiner Welt. Leo von Klenze, jener vielbeschäftige bayrische Architekt der ersten Hälfte des 19. Jahrhunderts, der die Antike zum höchsten Ideal seiner Kunst erhob, richtet sein Büro in München entsprechend ein. Formen und Farben sind im pompejanischen Stil gehalten, selbst die drei mit weißleinenen Rollos versehenen, zum Odeonsplatz ausgerichteten Fenster scheinen eher südliche denn bayrische Sonne in den Raum zu lassen.

typology of the artist's home instead of relating them to our present topic.

Considering the studio exclusively as a room within a preexisting structure the same demands apply as to the artist's house. Furnishings and decor should correspond to that which the architect wishes to communicate to clients—they should convey what he stands for, should mirror his tastes, his worldview. Leo von Klenze—a highly active Bavarian architect of the early nineteenth century who regarded antiquity as the highest ideal of art—furnished his studio in Munich accordingly. Forms and colors are in the Pompeian style, and even the three windows looking out onto Odeonsplatz are furnished with white linen blinds, seeming to admit a southern light into the room rather than a Bavarian one. Two shelves, upon which parade small antique sculptures, frame the large worktable, upon which the necessary

Zwei Regale, auf denen antike Kleinplastiken paradieren, rahmen den großen Arbeitstisch, auf dem die notwendigen Utensilien verstreut liegen. Zwei Stühle stehen bereit und laden, dank der wärmenden Teppiche, auch in der kalten Jahreszeit zum Arbeiten ein. Eigene Bilder Klenzes schmücken die Wände, eine nächste, große Ideallandschaft ist auf der Staffelei noch im Entstehen. Zum Power Napping lädt ein bequem anmutender Empire-Sessel ein – hier verdient der Fußwärmer besondere Aufmerksamkeit. Das Zimmer changiert zwischen Ordnung, die sich in den nach ihrer Größe aufgestellten Büchern manifestiert, und verhaltener künstlerischer Freiheit. Es entspricht somit ganz der Suche Klenzes nach einem der Antike folgenden, jedoch auch kreativ neuschöpfenden Stil.

Diese Übereinstimmung zwischen Atelier und persönlichem Stil entspricht der von Biografen und Historikern so gern gesehenen Einheit von Leben und Werk, die sich jedoch nicht selten als ein Trugbild erweist. Ist es letztlich nicht gleichgültig, wo gute Architektur entsteht? Ob in kreativer Unordnung zwischen Bergen von Modellen und Zeichnungen entstanden oder im klinisch reinen Architektur-Labor, Hauptsache sie ist gut! Im Chaos entsteht nicht zwingend chaotische Architektur, im Labor nicht unbedingt Präzision. In der umgenutzten Industriehalle wird nicht nur Industriearchitektur entworfen, auf dem Schiff oder dem Hausboot nicht nur Maritimes. Ist der Ort also zu vernachlässigen, kann Architektur überall entworfen werden? Die folgenden Beispiele bestätigen dies ebenso, wie sie es verneinen.

utensils lie dispersed. A pair of chairs stands at the ready, inviting the occupant to engage in his labors—even in the cold season, thanks to the warmth of the carpet. The walls are decorated with several paintings by Klenze himself—a large, ideal landscape, a work in progress, stands on an easel. A comfortable-looking Empire armchair proffers an invitation to power napping—here the foot warmer has received special attention. The room oscillates between the orderliness that is manifested in the books—arranged by size—and a kind of restrained artistic freedom. The whole corresponds, then, to Klenze's search for an innovative style that while creative, nonetheless follows antiquity.

This accord between studio and personal style corresponds to the unity of life and work which biographers and historians are so fond of discovering—and which is nonetheless often enough revealed to be an illusion. In the end, isn't it all the same where great architecture has its genesis? Whether created in disorder between heaps of models and drawings, or in a clinically pure architectural laboratory: the main thing is that it is good! Chaos does not necessarily produce chaotic architecture, a laboratory setting does not necessarily result in precision. Industrial architecture need not be designed in a converted factory hall; maritime design need not take place on a ship or houseboat. Is the workplace, then, of no importance? Can architecture be designed anywhere? The following examples simultaneously confirm and deny this assertion.

Alle Mann an Bord!

Das Künstlerhaus, in dem Leben und Arbeiten zu einer Einheit werden oder sich dialektisch widersprechen, hat eine bis in die Renaissance zurückreichende Tradition. Maler wie Andrea Mantegna, Universalkünstler wie Giulio Romano schufen sich Palazzi in Mantua. Nikodemus Tessins Stadtresidenz in Stockholm stand fürstlichen Palästen nicht nach, Friedrich Weinbrenners Haus in Karlsruhe spiegelte dessen Haltung in Reinform, Sir John Soanes Haus in London fasziniert durch seine unglaubliche Fülle an Ideen. In Brüssel ist Victor Hortas Palais das zentrale Beispiel seiner Architektur, Otto Wagner erfand sich mit seinen Wohnhäusern zweimal neu, was ebenso für Frank Lloyd Wright gilt. Die großen Meister der Moderne haben auch in Sachen Atelier die Themen und Räume vorgegeben. Auch hier finden wir oft die Übereinstimmung von Haus und architektonischer Haltung, so bei Konstantin Melnikows Atelierhaus in Moskau, bei Jean Prouvé in Nancy, Egon Eiermann in Baden-Baden und natürlich in Oswald Matthias Ungers mehrfach erweitertem Haus in Köln. Typenbildend waren jedoch, weil pragmatisch und überall preiswert zu mieten, schlichte Etagen, wie etwa diejenige von Mies van der Rohe in Chicago, oder – noch reduzierter – ein einfacher Schlauch.

Mitte der Zwanzigerjahre mietete Le Corbusier im 6. Arrondissement in Paris einen 50 Meter langen, 3,60 Meter breiten und knapp 4 Meter hohen Raum und betrieb dort gut vierzig Jahre lang sein Architekturatelier. Mal wird es als „elender Schlauch" (Wolfgang Pehnt) bezeichnet, mal als eine Galeere.

All on Board!

The artist's house—within which life and work merge to form a unity, or else contradict one another dialectically—enjoys a tradition that stretches all the way back to the Renaissance. Painters such as Andrea Mantegna and universal artists like Giulio Romano created palazzi in Mantua. Nikodemus Tessin's home in Stockholm ranked with princely palaces, and Friedrich Weinbrenner's house in Karlsruhe reflects his attitude in pure form. Sir John Soane's London house fascinates by virtue of an incredible abundance of ideas. In Brussels, Victor Horta's palais is a central exemplar of his architecture, while Otto Wagner reinvented himself twice through his homes—and the same is true of Frank Lloyd Wright. When it comes to the studio as well, the great masters of modernism prescribed themes and spaces. Here too, we frequently find a correspondence between house and architectural stance, instances of which include Konstantin Melnikov's studio house in Moscow, Jean Prouvé in Nancy, Egon Eiermann in Baden-Baden, and of course Oswald Matthias Ungers's multiple expanded house in Cologne. Also technologically formative—because pragmatic and leasable anywhere on economical terms—have been simple floors, such as those of Mies van der Rohe in Chicago, or—reduced even further—a simple tube.

In the mid-1920s, Le Corbusier rented a space measuring 50 meters in length, 3.6 meters in width, and 4 meters in height in the 6th arrondissement in Paris; he would maintain his architectural studio there for 40 years. The space has been referred to as a "wretched

Le Corbusiers dicht besetztes Atelier in der Rue de Sèvres, Paris
Le Corbusier's densely occupied studio on the rue de Sèvres, Paris

Le Corbusiers schmales Atelier in der Rue de Sèvres 35 hat nicht nur bei den Mitarbeitern Spuren hinterlassen. Auch den Meister selbst hat die besondere Raumerfahrung geprägt und sich in seinen Raumvorstellungen und seinem Proportionssystem, dem 1947 veröffentlichten *Modulor*, manifestiert. Kein Typus zwar, dennoch diente und dient dieser nüchterne Raum mit seiner klaren Sitzordnung und dem optimalen Seitenlicht als Vorbild. In unzähligen Abwandlungen taucht er immer wieder auf: Sei es ganz cool in helle Töne getaucht bei Bottega + Ehrhardts [S.54] Fabriketage in Stuttgart, sei es halb eingegraben in einem kleinen Waldstück, ebenfalls bestens belichtet und hell, in fein abgestimmten Farben, wie bei Selgascano [S.44] in Madrid.

Weniger Schlauch und mehr Galeere finden wir bei gmp [S.156], die sich schon früh ein eigenes, repräsentatives Bürogebäude in bester

tube" (Wolfgang Pehnt), but also as a galley. Le Corbusier's narrow studio at 35, rue de Sèvres has left its mark—and not only on his colleagues. This singular spatial experience also had an impact on the master himself, as reflected in his spatial conceptions and his proportional system, the *Modulor*, published in 1947. While representing no specific type, this austere room, with its clear seating arrangement and optimal lateral lighting, nonetheless served—and still serves—as a model. It surfaces again and again in countless variants: whether bathed, ultracool, in pale tones in Bottega + Ehrhardt's [p.54] factory floor in Stuttgart, or half-buried in a little wooded area, also optimally illuminated and adorned in pale, finely calibrated tones, in Selgascano [p.44] in Madrid.

We find ourselves less in a tube and more in a galley at gmp [p.156], a practice that was in a

Lage am noblen Hamburger Elbufer leisten konnten. Dabei sind es nicht die in der Postmoderne gern gewählten Schiffsmotive, sondern auch hier wieder die Sitzordnung, die eine Assoziation zur Galeere, dem kriegerischen Schiffstyp der Antike nahelegt. Zweireihig, streng hintereinander angeordnet sitzen die Mitarbeiter im nüchternen Stahlbau. Anders als im dunklen Schiffsrumpf unter Deck mag der schöne Blick für die langen Arbeitstage entschädigen. Und obwohl der Bildschirm schon lange den großen Zeichentisch mit Reißschiene und Lineal ersetzt und das von links kommende Seitenlicht längst nicht mehr zur optimalen Ausleuchtung des Arbeitstisches beiträgt, ist diese Anordnung nach wie vor in vielen, wenn nicht den meisten Architekturbüros anzutreffen. Wollen alle ein bisschen Le Corbusier sein und des großen Meisters Aura einfangen? Oder ist dieser sich hier abzeichnende Typus des Architekturateliers nur blankem Pragmatismus geschuldet, nämlich dem Angebot an bezahlbaren Büroräumen auf dem Markt? Wenn ja, dann schließt sich folgende Frage an.

Chaos oder Ordnung:
kreative Orte

Kann man anhand des Ateliers eines Architekten einen direkten Rückschluss auf dessen gebaute Architektur ziehen? Besonders bei den beiden folgenden Beispielen wird diese Vorstellung *ad absurdum* geführt, denn ob ein Architekt es bevorzugt, in seinem persönlichen Chaos oder an einem aufgeräumten Platz zu arbeiten, liegt neben seiner Arbeitsweise auch an seiner Ausbildung und seinem kulturellen Hintergrund.

position quite early on to afford its own prestigious office building at a prime location along the ritzy banks of the Elbe River in Hamburg. Here, it is not the ship motif so favored by postmodernism that evokes associations with the galley, but instead the seating arrangement, so suggestive of the military-style vessel of antiquity. In this businesslike steel building, colleagues sit in two rows, one set stringently behind the next. In contrast to life in a ship's dark hull, lovely views compensate somewhat for lengthy working days. And although the computer screen has long since supplanted the large drafting table with T-square and ruler, and lateral lighting from the left is no longer the optimal form of illumination for the workplace, this arrangement is still encountered in many—if not most—architectural offices. Perhaps all of them would like to be just a little bit like Le Corbusier, to capture something of the great master's aura? Or is the type of architectural studio that comes into focus here a function of sheer pragmatism, specifically the range of affordable office space currently available on the market? If so, then the following question arises.

Chaos or Order:
Creative Places

Can we draw any conclusions about the realized architecture of a given designer based on the look of his studio? In the two following examples in particular, this notion is pursued *ad absurdum,* for whether an architect prefers to work in personal chaos or in a tidy office is conditioned not just by his or her working approach, but by his or her training and cultural background as well.

Manche Ateliers versuchen, durch fast schon klinische Reinheit, glänzende Fluroberflächen und Neonröhren-Charme eine chirurgisch präzise Arbeitsweise zu vermitteln und gleichen dabei eher einem Krankenhausflur als einer Arbeitsstätte. Viele europäische Architekturbüros eifern darin den japanischen Architekten in ihrer konzeptuellen und „entwerferischen" Stringenz nach, sie bringen durch eine aufgeräumte Umgebung gedankliche Ordnung und Klarheit zum Ausdruck.

Denkt man bei japanischer Architektur an strengen Minimalismus, erwartet man kein Atelier, das mit einer unaufgeräumten Modellbauwerkstatt verwechselt werden könnte. Besonders auffallend am Büro von Sou Fujimoto Architects ist, wie wenig Raum der Mensch darin einnimmt. Er ist vollkommen von seiner Arbeit, seinen Entwurfsmodellen umgeben. Der Boden ist kaum noch sichtbar und nur ein vereinzelter Laptop deutet darauf hin, dass auch an Computern gearbeitet wird. Der Entwerfer kann sich in diesem Atelier völlig in seiner Arbeit verlieren, in ihr aufgehen und seinen Geist frei entfalten. Seine Umgebung diktiert ihm keine Perfektion, sondern Möglichkeiten und Spielräume.

Ein direkter Bezug zwischen Atelier und gebauter Architektur muss nicht immer offenkundig sein – vielleicht aber auf indirekte Weise ersichtlich. Wie Fujimoto in seiner Architektur versucht, die Grenzen zwischen Innen und Außen aufzulösen, wird in seinem Atelier versucht, die sture Zeichenarbeit und den Modellbau zu vereinen. Dieses Atelier dient nicht als Aushängeschild des Architekten, denn am Ende des Entwurfsprozesses

Some studios attempt—by means of an almost clinical cleanliness, gleaming corridors, and the charm emanated by fluorescent lighting—to convey a surgically precise approach, and hence come to resemble a hospital ward or workstation. In their conceptual and design stringency, many European architectural offices emulate Japanese architects, whose well-ordered surroundings are an expression of conceptual order and clarity.

If the mention of Japanese architecture evokes severe minimalism—one hardly expects a studio that could be confused with a messy model-building workshop. Particularly striking in the office of Sou Fujimoto Architects is how little space he actually takes up. He is completely surrounded by his work, by his design models. The floor is almost invisible, and only a single laptop alludes to the fact that some work is performed on computer as well. In this studio, the designer can lose himself entirely in his work, becoming absorbed in it; his intellect can develop without constraint. His surroundings dictate not perfection, but possibilities, room for maneuver.

A direct connection between studio and realized architecture need not necessarily be evident—yet it may perhaps instead be observable in an oblique way. Just as Fujimoto seeks in his architecture to dissolve the boundary between interior and exterior, an attempt is made in his studio to unify stubborn drafting work and model building. This studio serves not as the architect's flagship, for at the end of the design process, it is not a question of order or chaos in the workplace itself, but instead of the architecture that has its genesis there.

Das Büro von Sou Fujimoto gleicht einer großen Modellbauwerkstatt.
The office of Sou Fujimoto resembles a large model-building workshop.

geht es nicht um Ordnung oder Chaos vor Ort, sondern um die Architektur, die dort entsteht.

Kein Atelier gleicht dem anderen, eine Typologie zeichnet sich nicht ab. Wenn auch in jedem Architektenatelier mehr oder weniger dasselbe stattfindet, so setzen die einen mehr auf Funktionalität, die anderen mehr auf Repräsentation. Dabei kann sich die architektonische Haltung im Atelier spiegeln und kann die Raumerfahrung im Atelier die architektonische Idee beeinflussen, aber es kann auch genau das Gegenteil der Fall sein. Herrscht im Büro Chaos, so müssen die Bauten, die darin geplant werden, nicht chaotisch sein. Kreativität setzt keinen spezifischen Ort voraus, wenn auch das landläufige Bild eines Künstlerateliers von kreativer Unordnung geprägt ist. Architekten sind aber eine besondere Sorte von Künstlern und der Ort, an dem sie arbeiten, ist etwas anderes als ein Künstleratelier: Er changiert zwischen Labor, Kommunikationsort, technischem Büro, Ausstellung, *studiolo* und Klause. Was aber geschieht, wenn es gar keinen festen, physischen Ort mehr gibt?

Das ubiquitäre Büro

Wie weit beeinflussen sich Entwurfsraum und Raumentwurf? Entwerfen mobile Architekten mobile Architektur? Immobilie – *im mobilis* versus *mobilis*?

Versuchte Bruno Munari 1950 in der Fotoserie *Seeking comfort in an uncomfortable armchair* eine adäquate Leseposition in einem modernen Lehnstuhl zu finden, so propagierte Hans Hollein 1969 im *Mobilen*

No studio resembles another; no typology manifests itself. And if more or less the same sorts of things go on in every architectural studio, then one nonetheless sets more store in functionality, another in prestige functions. It may be that a given practice of architectural orientation is mirrored in its studio, that the way in which space is experienced there can influence architectural ideas—but then again, the contrary may also be the case. Chaos may reign in the studio, but this by no means suggests that the buildings planned there will be chaotic. And even if the popular image of the artist's studio is one of creative chaos, creativity in fact presupposes no specific location. The architect, however, is a very special kind of artist, and his or her workplace differs markedly from the studios of fine artists: it oscillates between laboratory, communication center, technical office, place of exhibition, *studiolo*, and retreat. But what happens when it no longer occupies a fixed abode, a physical location?

The Ubiquitous Office

To what extent do the design space and the design of space influence each other? Do mobile architects design mobile architecture?

In 1950, in the photo series *Seeking Comfort in an Uncomfortable Armchair*, Bruno Munari sought to define an adequate reading position for the modern armchair, and in 1969, in his *Mobilen Büro* (mobile office), Hans Hollein propagated the liberation from the context of a fixed workplace structure—temporary work activity with drafting table and telephone in an inflatable room. Meanwhile, technical and

**anOtherArchitect bei einem Architektur-
seminar in Kirgistan**
anOtherArchitect at an architecture seminar
in Kyrgyzstan

**Das FutureCityLab in Berlin erarbeitet urbane
Visionen für das Jahr 2050.**
The FutureCityLab in Berlin elaborates urban
visions for the year 2050.

Kaffee und urbane Forschung in Jaroslawl
Coffee and urban research in Yaroslavl

Büro die Befreiung vom Kontext einer festen Arbeitsplatzstruktur – temporäres Arbeiten mit Reißbrett und Telefon im aufblasbaren Raum. Die avantgardistische Design-Performance und die architektonische Inszenierung sind durch die technische und digitale Entwicklung inzwischen Realität. Die *Wolke* des Wolf D. Prix, die *Idee, Architektur veränderbar wie Wolken zu bauen,* findet sich zeitgenössisch wörtlich und transformiert in der *Cloud.*

Die zunehmende Komplexität und Simultanität verlangt nach OpenSource Strategien, Clouds, Smart Phones und Tablets, Digital Devices, Services und Apps, und offeriert

digital developments have made avant-garde design performance and architectural staging a reality. Currently, Wolf D. Prix's Cloud—the idea of building an architecture that is alterable, like a cloud—is being transformed literally into the *cloud.*

A growing complexity and simultaneity calls for open-source strategies, clouds, smart phones and tablets, digital devices, services, and apps, and offers a new architectural design structure. Mies van der Rohe's modernist credo *less is more* has lost its relevance; valid today is the idea *more is more.* The new simplicity lies in complexity.

**Modelle unter Palmen in der Outdoor-Werkstatt
von Studio Mumbai**
Models under palm trees in the outdoor workshop
of Studio Mumbai

eine neue architektonische Entwurfsstruktur. Das moderne Credo *weniger ist mehr* von Mies van der Rohe hat seine Bedeutsamkeit verloren, heute gilt *mehr ist mehr.* Die neue Einfachheit liegt in der Komplexität.

Ein *anOtherArchitect* tritt in Erscheinung. Daniel Dendra zeigt repräsentativ die neuen Möglichkeiten, Architektur zu entwerfen, zu diskutieren und zu realisieren. Momentaufnahmen und Einblicke in seinen Alltag bilden einen Kontrast zur klassischen Architekturfotografie und selbstdarstellerischen Dokumentation von Architekten. Als *anOtherArchitect* definiert und entwirft Daniel Dendra Architektur als Prozess und Struktur via kollaborativer Plattform,

anOtherArchitect emerges. Daniel Dendra exemplifies the new possibilities for designing, discussing, and realizing architecture. Snapshots and insights into his everyday activities provide a contrast to classical architectural photography, to the self-publicizing documentation of architects. As anOtherArchitect, Daniel Dendra defines architecture as process and structure via collaborative platforms, opensource design, cloudscape, and FutureCityLab. Furnishings are minimal: analog with pen and paper, digital with laptop, charge adapter, wireless Internet, and espresso to go. He is always on the move, a modern nomad in international airports, air-conditioned conference rooms, hotel breakfast rooms, in a tent, and under